The Hate Poems

OTHER BOOKS BY JOHN TOTTENHAM

The Inertia Variations

Antiepithalamia & Other Poems of Regret and Resentment

The Hate Poems

John Tottenham

WITH AN INTRODUCTION
BY LOUIS PIPE

LOS ANGELES

Cover design by Derek Martin & Leanna Robinson
Typography by Derek Martin
Drawings by John Tottenham

Published by Amok Books
Los Angeles, California

First Edition

ISBN: 1-878923-29-3

ISBN13: 978-1878923-29-5

Amok Books are available to bookstores through our primary distribu-
tor: SCB Distributors, 15608 South New Century Drive, Los Angeles,
CA 90248. Phone: 800-729-6423, 310-532-9400. Fax: 310-532-7001.
Home page: www.scbdistributors.com.

UK Distributors: Turnaround Distribution, Unit 3, Olympia Trading
Estate, Coburg Road, Wood Green, London N22 6TZ.
Phone: (0181) 829 3000. Fax: (0181) 881 5088.
Home page: http://www.turnaround-uk.com

To view the complete Amok Books catalog,
please go to www.amokbooks.com.

CONTENTS

to Angel Baby

Introduction

When I was asked to write a foreword to this volume my first impulse was to decline, believing as I do that if you can't find anything nice to say about something, why say anything at all - a sentiment that is clearly not shared by the author. Then I agreed, providing that anything I had to say should be included as an afterword, not a foreword.

As an early champion of this late-blooming talent (my laudations also adorned his last collection and some further observations were included in my recent volume of essays on contemporary poetry*), I have closely tracked his slow and desultory progress—admittedly, not a very time-consuming task—from 'belated start to premature conclusion,' and I cannot escape the feeling that the 'poims' contained herein display a substantial drop in quality from those in his previous two volumes. Upon reading the manuscript my initial reaction was one of distaste and disappointment: reactions that the author seems to invite, although perhaps not to such a dispiriting extent.

These 'Hate Poems' suggest a poet who has exhausted his meager fund of subject matter and written himself into a rather dusty and squalid corner. Facilitated by a disingenuous safety valve of self-deprecation, he is now scraping - and sharing - the dregs. An early title that was considered and subsequently rejected by the author was, in fact, 'The Dregs', and a most apposite one it would have been. Eventually he went with the equally appropriate 'Hate Poems', as he says, "...to grab people's attention with a simple, declarative, negative title. It's an obvious title, but surprisingly, nobody's ever used it before. I hate the title, I hate the reason for using it, and I am deeply ambivalent regarding the contents."** Fair enough.

Containing the cream (the dregs) of his poetic work amassed between the publication of his last slender collection of verse— 'Antiepithalamia & Other Poems of Regret and Resentment' (2012)—

8

and 2015, at which point, to his credit, he stopped writing poetry entirely, not only do these poims address staleness, they actually are stale, and they attest to a decrease of the redemptive accessibility that distinguished the author's earlier works. Having mostly abandoned the universal 'I' that he claimed was his chosen province—"to write as impersonally as possible, while bringing as much personal experience to it as possible"**—here, with these morbid, spiteful 'unclean offerings,' he descends at times into rancorous and cloying self-pity as he explores his own distinctive malaise: that of an artist who left it too late, and love poems with the emphasis on hate. Were he not such an obscure and unprolific figure he would by now have become a self-parody. As Nietzsche observed, "The crowd will not cry 'Hosanna' until you ride into town on an ass," and that is what Tottenham seems to be attempting here by brazenly pandering to the 'haters' and the kitten-loving hordes.

Nevertheless (or "always the less," as the author would have it), a work of art should speak for itself and it should be measured against its own ambitions, and here the author succeeds, for if nothing else, he has a distinct voice that contains few other echoes, and, as he says, "An unseemly surge of late-blooming ambition, now dried up, was not enough to save me."

Despite the aforementioned reservations, these poims still rise above most anything else I'm aware of out there in the world of contemporary poitry (not that I'm familiar with much else that is out there), and if on occasion Tottenham repeats himself (an over-reliance on the word 'numb' is impossible to ignore - but it is a word that doesn't have many synonyms and the condition is addressed with great frequency), he is no more guilty of that tendency than anyone else. Poets are doomed, among other fates, to repeating themselves. Another inevitable fate, of course, is to be consigned to a world of embittered obscurity, and this is the world that Tottenham restlessly inhabits and relentlessly explores.

By definition, what is a poet? Somebody who uses language well - so well that it can be set on separate lines on a page and withstand pedantic scrutiny; whose felicitous phrasing might even provide the reader with pleasure. By which token, Tottenham is definitely a poet. If these verses were set to music he would be considered one of the finest songwriters of our time, but verses without music don't command much appreciation these days. Ironically, to call an artist or a filmmaker a poet—i.e. 'Lou Reed is a poet,' 'Tarkovsky is a poet of the cinema,' &c— is to bestow the highest honor upon them, but if one actually is a poet, one is a nobody, and if one writes with clarity in a style that is accessible to people who don't read poetry—i.e. everybody—then one is less than a nobody, one is a martyr to a lost cause. And that is the dilemma that Tottenham faces, and that the critic is faced with when confronted with his work.

This new collection, 'The Hate Poems', presents a further elaboration on the themes addressed in his two earlier volumes - 'The Inertia Variations' and 'Antiepithalamia'. In elegantly-wrought laments of self-deprecation and mean-spirited love poems, the author finds that he has more to say on already exhausted subjects, and gives voice to the kind of thoughts most people prefer not to express but will nevertheless automatically relate to and be entertained by. As Maurice Blanchot said: "Optimists write badly. But pessimists do not write at all." Tottenham has staked out a singular terrain where egotism and self-loathing meet, where futility merges with urgency, and beauty is created out of bitterness. If nothing else, he furnishes proof that a poet maudit can still, if not thrive, at least survive, alive and unwell, in this benighted age, and that the dregs can sometimes be the cream.

Louis Pipe,
Lubbock, Texas 2018

* *Rhetoric Of Inconvenience: Lyrical Strategies In The New Millennium (University of West Texas Press, 2015)*

** Interview with the author, 2018

Share the
Se,lfishness

'A collection of such pieces only as may be received in a virtuous court, and may not unbecome the cabinet of the severest matron.'

Every word carefully weighed.

A RICHER VICTORY

Broke, bitter and alone.
What more could I possibly ask for?
I have failed, at last,
beyond my wildest expectations.
I don't understand
why I'm still not satisfied.

LIFE'S JOURNEY

I seemed to have always been the same age.
Then I looked in the mirror and saw a tired
and devious old man gazing warily back at me:

An old man, sitting alone in a room,
masturbating over a memory,
fantasizing about women
who have forgotten about me,
and brooding
over deliberately missed opportunities.

A shadow of my former shadow
slowly becoming invisible, turning gray.
Unfortunately, nobody noticed
that I never went away.

GOLDEN WATERS

Instead of doing my own work,
I took a long hard look
at somebody else's work,
in the hope of being pleasantly relieved
by how bad it was.
But, much as I tried to deny it,
it was undeniably good.
And it pours out of him
like a gusher from a golden fountain
that never stops flowing.
Compared to this strained trickle
from a blocked and rusty faucet.
I take consolation
in how much it has cost me,
as if that somehow redeems it.
Which, of course, it doesn't.
But I don't have much else
to take consolation in.

BEAUTY AND HAPPINESS

Beauty depresses me,
knowing that it's temporary.
Positivity requires too much energy.
And even if I were happy,
I wouldn't admit it,
for that would be an insult
to those who are not,
and those who pretend to be.

STAGNATION PARTY

You watch other people losing it
and you wonder if it could happen to you.
It could.
You swagger in vain
against extinction. But the efforts of those
who wrest crumbs from history won't be enough
to ensure your immortality.
You might have done more
had others done less, had you not been thwarted
by the unsightly spectacle of other people's success.
You were guilty of the conceit of the refusal
to compete, good enough not to have to prove it.
You lacked the nerve, the brazen importunity,
and you resent those who wisely used
the time and opportunities you abused.
But at least you failed deliberately,
or so you insist.
You watch other people lose it
and you wonder if it can happen to you.
It can.
Maybe it already has.

DON'T LOOK BACK

I lie down and let it pour through me:
The pain of love taken, and then taken away.
The pain of love not given.
You gave me love; you killed me with kindness,
then just killed me.

In the pleated shade of your comforting unworldliness,
time stood still.
I forgot that clouds moved,
I forgot the smell of new-cut grass.
And now I can no longer behold beauty
without contemplating loss.

I tried to dismiss the past,
and also failed at self-forgiveness.
Sunk by a ballast of unconditional love,
I forgot the sea's indifference.

STAGE FRIGHT

What if you woke up one morning
toward the end of this life in progress
to discover that this was it, the main event,
not a rehearsal, not another period of transition,
but that the curtain is about to fall
after an endless intermission;
that all this time that seemed like preparation
was in fact culmination, and prelude
headed straight into decline;
if you looked ahead to find -
after a lifetime of sordid cares and unclean offerings,
and imagining that real life was waiting in the wings -
that the life you thought you had been building up to
is no longer possible, that this is it,
and it's almost over?

MY LATE STYLE

There no longer seems to be much point
in pointing out the pointlessness.
It hardly seems worth lamenting anymore.
After all this talk of giving up, just do it.
Don't worry. Nobody will notice.

BEYOND A DEAD HORSE

You always seemed displeased with me,
and I always seemed bored by you.
I idealized you when you weren't around
and didn't appreciate you when you were.
You were always there
and I was always elsewhere:
in a parallel universe
of what I'd rather be doing,
who I'd rather be screwing.
Now you're somewhere else,
and I'm still here;
and now that I don't have you,
I don't want anybody else.

INCAPABLE IDEALS

This compulsive need to 'actualize' myself
has consumed far too much of my being.
I wish I could divest myself
of this tiresome illusion
that I have something to offer.
It would make it so much easier
for everybody concerned.
Not that anybody else is concerned.

GLUE TRAP

Now that I'm stuck alone in the glue trap
that we tumbled into together,
and from which you nimbly extricated yourself,
I'm going to have to pay for the fact
that we were once in the same place at the same time.

Killing loneliness with emptiness
consumes too much time and energy. Dull security
seems preferable at this point. Compromise
is for the wise. Resign yourself to satisfaction,
and remember how precious
the boredom will seem in retrospect.

All the old pain has taken too long to fade.
There's not much time left for new pain to fade.
It took all these years to figure out
that I'm not suited for relationships.
Great: Now I can spend my old age alone
and die a lonely death.

BEFORE THE FACT

I have mixed feelings about it.
It seems like the sensible option,
and it would certainly make a nice change.
On the other hand, I have some concerns
about incompetence and pain;
and despite elaborate fantasies to the contrary,
posthumous glory is highly unlikely.
At this late stage, the negatives still outweigh the positives.
But mainly I'm holding back in order
to deny some people the satisfaction
of congratulating themselves
on their prescience.

UNDELIVERANCE

I recognize the ideal,
of what I'm ideally working towards,
but I'm incapable of realizing it.
So why not satisfy myself
with what I imagine
I'm capable of doing
rather than actually doing it?
That seems like a reasonable solution.

But isn't that what I've been doing all along:
recognizing what I'm capable of
and settling for less?
The long process
of resigning oneself to failure:
basking in the glory of potential
and potential glory,
until potential is ingloriously dead.

SUCK SORROW

You ended it,
but I laid all the groundwork,
and now I feel that a weight has lifted
but I want the weight back.
I miss the continual thin drizzle
of our conversation, your cold softness,
and the unmistakably sour whiff
of your nocturnal flatulence
as we lay clinging to each other
in your suffocatingly overheated bedroom.
Impaled on tender memories,
run through on spikes of regret,
spurting up sadness; penetrated
and haunted; the novelty of feeling something
is refreshing, even if it is sorrow: mourning
the loss of something I never wanted.

THE INDIFFERENT SUBLIME

Immerse yourself in sorrow, rake over pain.
Let the novelty of feeling something
wash through you in purifying waves
again and again. But kindness is unnerving,
tenderness hurts, and empathy
can be an excruciating form of martyrdom.
At the end of the day - when all is unsaid
and undone - you're better off numb.

FINITE SITUATION

When one talks about it in advance,
it sounds weak, unconvincing and trite,
like this. Only when numb, which is most of the time,
does it seem inviting: when I can't tell the difference
between the pleasure of feeling nothing
and the horror of not feeling anything.
I like myself too much or something.
But perhaps that shouldn't be considered an obstacle.
Of course, none of us would be here if it wasn't painful.
But still, I'm afraid that it will take me by surprise;
maybe tonight, maybe another day.
My last sunrise. It doesn't matter.
I never watched the sun rise anyway.

FRESH FAILURE

I could have been
ahead of my time;
I could have been
me.
Nevertheless, I proceed,
directionlessly,
hoping to profit
from useless hard-won knowledge,
and brooding about mortality -
about how depressing it is
that nobody knows my name,
and how inconvenient
that one has to die
in order to receive posthumous acclaim.
And worse still, that one
has to have accomplished something.

I must put that on my to-do list.
But what are you going to do
when the life you passively awaited
has slowly passed you by?
You can't hate something
because you made it unattainable,
and you can't resent other people
because you let yourself down.
But you can try.

AN UNORIGINAL OBSERVATION

By the time one has learned how to live,
there isn't much time left to profit
from what one has learned.

And it's too late to still be learning,
too late to still be burning,
to come to terms with the past
by learning the easiest things last.

GET LUCKY

The night is young. But I am old:
Three years older,
three years less desirable.
After a long stretch of being
one half of a couple, one half of myself,
a sour thirst for a satisfying revulsion
renews itself.

Time stands still when you're in a relationship.
It dies in its sleep, beneath a threadbare security blanket.
You wake up, weakened: three years have passed.
Those windows that were once cracked slightly open
are now shut tight. The curtains are drawn,
dust blows across the floor, and the kittens
aren't coming to the saucer of milk anymore.

And the milk has soured. During that age of suspension,
you didn't pay much attention to your dwindling allure,
which, lacking wealth or fame, beyond a certain age,
is assured. Now it is clear that your standards
are going to have to fall
even further. Maybe, if you get lucky,
some poor lost soul might get desperate enough
to return your call.

LIFE WITHOUT LIMITS

I can feel time passing me by,
speeding up as I slow down,
creating the kind of deceptive, reflexive glory
that occurs when the speed of the past
overtakes the slowed down present.

I was riding into the promise
of a life without limits,
boundlessly rich with possibilities,
when the future suddenly turned into the past -
and looking back,
it wasn't hugely satisfying.

All this time always seemed to be leading somewhere,
but it never went anywhere.
The past established itself as the future dried up;
markers appeared and as chronology fell into place,
events that once seemed insignificant became milestones.

It all already happened, those were the times.
All my fantasies are memories now,
as are most of my realities,
and all I'm looking back on is anticipation.

UNDIMINISHED

From now on I'm going to be a shadow
of my former shadow:
Living in the present, negligibly,
and regretting the past, sweepingly.
As for the future, I'm not sure if I have one.
But I've been saying that for a long time,
and I'm still here,
even if I am ten years behind my time.
Make that fifteen.

THE ONE

I am the one
waiting for the One.

I have never entered a room
without hoping that the One
I am waiting for
might be found there.

Despite decades of disappointment,
I still look for it in every face,
looking for somebody to become that place
where everything that falls apart
falls into place.

But if I found her, I wouldn't want her,
for as long as the possibility
of somebody else wanting me exists,
I will always want somebody else.

And I realize now that if she ever does arrive
it will not be in the prime of either of our lives,
at a cocktail party with a drink in her hand,
but that she is more likely to arrive holding a bedpan
as I am breathing my last in a hospital bed.

Only then, with restlessness and hope extinguished,
and all other options exhausted,
will I finally be ready
for the One.

INSPIRED BY TRUE EVENTS

Out of loyalty to perversity,
I made a commitment
to unrepentant fatalism.
I devoted myself to dissent and deprivation,
imagining, in my boundless optimism,
that others had done the same.

But as the years groan by,
the wide-open solipsism of youth yields
to the more insidious solipsism of middle-age,
and they give up or grow up, my contemporaries.
Inevitably, the time to show their hand arrives:
to reveal what they've been holding,
or withholding, all along.
The mythic lift gives way
to the staggered decline.
And I find that I am quite alone
in the stance I have taken,
that I have committed myself
only to a lost cause.

But is it not an achievement of sorts
to maintain fidelity to the values of one's youth,
when one's vision is supposedly at its most pure?
It must, at least, be a sort of success.
It is, at least, the only sort of success
that I can make any claim on.
Though it could have been achieved in finer style.

SAY YOU LOVE ME

"I love you," she says,
and my heart sinks.
Knowing what is required of me,
I attempt to reciprocate.
But it's a struggle,
the words won't take shape.
No other phrase is so hard to articulate;
no other sentiment is voiced so apprehensively.
I could be honest and say: I love you
but almost everything about you annoys me...
But somehow
those three precious, perilous syllables
are squeezed out, squeamishly:
"Isle... of you."
It never sounds right when I say it,
but I say it
to put her at ease,
because what you get out of it,
temporarily,
is peace.

THE CREATIVE PROCESS

The moment slipping away,
sinking into the unseizable day.
The sapping sun, the sadness
kept at bay, the churlish thoughts
that are allowed to circle freely,
while clinging
to a perverted form of integrity.
A threadbare urgency,
as pointless as poetry
but tighter than time.

THE END IS NEAR HERE

Because I'm thinking about it,
does that mean I'm contemplating it?
I take it for granted that I take it
for granted, but I never genuinely
contemplate it. One toys with it in advance,
leaving it, finally, up to chance, a blur
of which one must beware, long past hope;
when velleity becomes volition, crushed
by the weight of a whisper; l'esprit d'escalier
at the end of a rope, at the end of the end
of this endless reprieve, with no time left to relish
the nasty stain one's life will leave.

I can't decide if I am justified
in parting with these memories,
no longer mine, shared with nobody.
It doesn't seem like much of a bargain:
to exchange everything for nothing;
to discover that nothing feels
like nothing on earth.
The more I recognize my fate,
the more I recognize my worth.

TIME UNREGAINED

At this point it would be impossible
to make up for all the lost time.
I might as well try to settle
for a serviceable desperation,
and strive, at least, for resignation:
the long hard process of resigning myself
to the choices I made
by not making a choice.

ALL DOWN THE LINE

Passing the various stations,
the vicarious stations,
watching the other passengers get off,
without baggage, at the earliest stop -
once they feel they've done their time,
but still they want credit for riding
to the end of the line.
And at the terminal, what awaits?
Just a faded ticket, out of date.

ALWAYS TORN, NEVER BORN

Some former curmudgeons, later in life,
make a conscious decision to become warm
and encompassing individuals.
As mortality becomes more tangible,
they realize it's a waste of rapidly diminishing time
to be cagey and mean-spirited, and with an effort,
no less laudable for being discernible,
they summon long-buried reserves of warmth
and generosity. They realize that it's time
to be a good person, and strive towards that end
until it comes naturally.

Such a position, however, requires financial
(and sometimes connubial) well-being:
a secure center from which geniality and generosity
can flow outward. It can be a heroic feat
and is probably very rewarding for all concerned.
Unfortunately, I am incapable of it on a practical level,
as I cannot financially (or connubially) afford it.

BURNT OUT ON THE SUN

Gazing up into the hills, at the sunlight
flashing through the palm trees, reality blurs
and I wonder what became of the last twenty years -
in this town of tits and teeth,
of slow power and soft atmosphere.

Is it better to dry up in the land of dreams
or dream in the land of the dried-up,
to exchange grim reality for feckless heliolatry -
a soothing, beguiling and insidious softness?

There is safety in numbness,
in so denatured a locality, so far removed
from nature and history.
And I'm deeply grateful, to be stuck here,
sinking in geographical and cultural isolation,
seldom jolted out of numbness
in this seductively deadening place,
both sanctuary and termination.

LIQUID CONSOLATION AND KNOB RELIEF

While we make polite conversation,
exchanging veiled vanities,
I stare at the pale blue leaf-like veins of your hand
and imagine those long thin delicate fingers
that now tenderly stroke the slender stem of a wine glass, wrapped
around my flagging manhood;
and those soft ethereal lips,
that take modest sips of wine,
clamped hungrily around it.
I hope that the gleam in your eyes
means that something potent, painful
and profound is ready to be released
once enough has taken place above
and below the surface of this longing.
And that this moment won't go the way
of all the other unseized moments.

IMPERFECT DAY

Outside, a sparrow sits on the telegraph wire,
a stray dog limps across the sidewalk.
And that is the extent of nature in these parts.
Silence drills through me, birdsong flickers in the air,
overlaid by the constant drone of traffic and tinnitus.
Urgency fades into futility, and once again I find myself
on the verge of giving up before I have even begun.
If I could see myself sitting here:
a benumbed idealist, a lazy perfectionist,
barely engaged in the pretense of activity,
I don't know whether I'd laugh or cry...
or remain numb.

LETTING GO

In a constant state of choking down bitterness.
Getting it all down in the hope of exhausting it.
Only to find there's more, it multiplies.

How empty my life would be without it.
What a gaping hole it would leave.
And what could possibly take its place?

That's a good question...
I'm drawing a blank.

To 'let go' of bitterness and resentment:
It's an interesting concept.
I must try it sometime.
No hurry.

THE COMING MAN

Revulsion rushes in
as the last spasms subside.
And in the afterglow, filled
with the futility of the act,
far from the fevers
that preceded the flood,
the seed of indifference
trickles down your back.
How foolish and pointless
it all suddenly seems.
I only wish I felt this way
in my dreams.

DEATH IN THE HILLS

So these are the pleasures of conversation at the big table,
among the best, the most ambitious, the most willing
to play the game. We, the successful, have found each other.
Now we can be ourselves, and drop bigger names.

The talk is about who's who and who knows who,
about people who never give a second thought to you:
a rich variety of bores and names that open doors,
used as currency in a chain of connections
linked by fragile egos.

Find the most famous person in the room,
attach yourself to them and start name-dropping:
that is the accepted formula. Meanwhile, ration yourself out
according to the eminence of your interlocutor.

Oiled for a smooth round of social intercourse,
my neighbor continually peers over my shoulder,
seeking a more deserving drain for his social juices.
Cast further adrift by this subtle urgency,
I can feel my precious life ebbing away.
Better to be a recluse than a loose wreck,
a small fish in a pond instead of lost at sea.
Erudition without motivation cuts no ice around here;
the extent of my ambition is shabby gentility.

Success is the perfect disguise for sycophancy,
and an effectual mask for insecurity.
Nobody can accuse you of being a climber
when you're already at the top.
And it never stops:
Sustaining the illusion of engagement
by pretending to be interested in things
that one will immediately forget.
It's a different need at a different speed:
moving swiftly, knowingly, in shallow waters,
beneath waves of polished insincerity.

I can go from biting loneliness
to social claustrophobia - and back -
in ten seconds flat.
Terrorized by polite conversation,
I don't have much energy,
and I don't have much appetite
for other people's energy.
Groaning inwardly, aching for silence, I can feel
my precious hours bleeding into slowly measured death,
devoured by people who ignore me. I could bite
the hand that feeds, but it isn't very nourishing,
and it would be spat back.

Facing a firing squad, without blindfold, or billfold.
The ammunition is blind ambition,
from a machine gun loaded with bullets of pretension
that unfortunately don't kill you.
They're looking for bigger game while firing blanks.
This barrage of frighteningly unconvincing positivity
and overheard flattery is draining and ultimately depressing.
So much urgency when so little is at stake.
Maybe if they gave me more attention,
it would be easier
to take.

SENSE AND INSENSIBILITY

You fell just far enough
to break your fall, losing it
while being careful not to lose it all.
A struggle embraced conditionally,
that you could emerge from victoriously,
with enhanced credibility.

It got tired, being totally wired.
Excess was proof of vitality,
a form of insurance, a passage
to integrity that wouldn't
otherwise come naturally.
Carelessness was calculation,
a graceful camouflage for ambition,
wrapped in adversity. You yearned
to earn the right to have your problems
taken seriously, to move on
and claim your reward:
the right to be bored.

Your own personal Calvary. Rising again,
demanding adoration and respect
for having survived massive pleasure.
Singled out for glory, as if it were heroic
or holy. Sensation dulled
into group-sanctioned security.
A way of paying your dues,
to wear your demons as a badge of honor
or another tattoo.

Once you'd had enough
of doing all the best stuff,
it became your moral duty
to exploit your precious tragedy,
to grab it and milk it dry,
and hug yourself with delight in the camera eye.
You don't have to live the life anymore
but by the grace of your well-timed fall
you can encourage others to get into it
for the long haul.

The new you is even more about you:
you have gone, you have grown
from indulging yourself destructively
to indulging yourself protectively,
from letting your senses run riot
to yoga, meditation and a vegan diet,
and, most importantly, avoiding
your former comrades. That jig is up.
Now you worship the empty bottle,
not the full cup.

LEFT HANGING

A gifted young man is dead. Too bad
that it wasn't somebody else instead.
A dysfunctional immortality awaits him.
It's shocking, saddening, comforting
to find that somebody so successful
is capable of doing himself in.
It's haunting, his tragedy makes
the prospect of one's own end less daunting.
A few weeks later, however, the autopsy determines
death by misadventure.
It was only auto-erotic asphyxiation.
How disappointing.

ELLA G.

Lost in thought, or simply lost,
you sat on the curb, smoking
your first cigarette of the day
as the early morning traffic streamed by.
You seemed at one with being at odds
with your surroundings.
And I sat behind you, unnoticed,
charmed and slightly envious.

You already looked like a ghost,
then you disappeared
and returned like a shadow, clearly
out of reach. You looked away
when we passed each other on the street.
Then you disappeared again,
and your life was complete.

EARTH

How dark and wide and wet it was:
pungent in the morning,
with steam rising from it.
I held my nose over it,
breathed in deeply
and gagged.

A hole, deeper than my love,
awaited you. A shallow hole,
nonetheless.

WINDSONG

I have a heart like a wheelbarrow,
there are no windmills in my mind.
Love blows in and floats around freely
like the wind - getting in the way
of other things.

This rootless love without design,
which has no object, point or point of origin -
one looks for it in every face,
looking for somebody to become that place
where everything that falls apart
falls into place.

It seeks definition, a place of rest,
to find its home in a woman's breast -
to die there, or multiply there.
When, surely, to keep it to oneself
would be best.

NAP ON A MUGGY AFTERNOON

When we part, all the closeness and pleasure
of our time together immediately dissolves
into lonely agitation. Having shared a cool iron bed
with a warm and beautiful woman, I return home
and lie incapacitated on the sofa: drained, dismantled,
wracked with longing and restlessness;
yet somehow, despite the dismal aftereffects,
it seems worth it.

DRAIN IN VAIN

An acute sensation of falling
for and into a black hole,
a soft focus abyss, otherwise known as bliss.
Or a train wreck, carrying hazardous waste,
something I can look forward to
looking back on with distaste.

Constantly fighting funny familiar feelings of futility,
trying to put the brakes on the morbidity,
but it keeps rolling down the line.
And as I watch it disappear,
life as I have long known it,
becomes all the more precious
and acutely defined.

AN ALLIANCE OF SORTS

Is this the real thing or dull desperation?
The last frontier or the last resort?
Something to take comfort in,
complain about, or both?
The purity of impotence
or ceremonial suffocation?
I suppose it could be worse:
There are worse things than love,
there are worse things than constipation.
Let's just try to make the most
of a bad situation.

THE POET'S COCK

I hoped that I had grown
too old and jaded for this sort of thing.
Wrong again: a form of madness.
Persevering until it glows with white heat
and elixirates a delicate foam of sadness.

It's sensitizing, of course,
to feel this way,
and ideally it should nurture
other areas of one's life like gentle rain.
But this sort of happiness feels
like a dead end. Bliss:
but I would still be relieved
were it to end.
No problem:
That can be arranged.

PILLOW TALK

I know I've underestimated you in the past,
and thought of you as vacuous,
but that's because you were unavailable.
Now that you're compliant,
I see you as you really are:
as spiritually beautiful
as you are in the flesh.

Just when I thought myself
out of charm's way, the familiar cycle
of pining and suffocation resumes:
floating in an elated daze
into an overcast, jagged terrain,
where sweetness and simplicity
get sour and skewed.

As I meet the melting loveliness in your eyes,
I worry weakly about compromise
and feminine wiles. I fell hard
because you pushed softly.
There was bound to be an impact;
and having observed the untidy results,
you are surely now questioning your wisdom.

As you cling to me affectionately,
covering me with tender kisses,
I visualize you, in great detail,
melting beneath the thrusts of another,
and imagine how much I'll miss you,
once I've finally succeeded in alienating you.

HOOKED ON A FEELING

I marvel at my feelings,
but I don't trust them.
I'm dazzled by her,
but I don't trust her either.
I'm not sure that she even likes me.
Which is fine, I don't like her much either.

DEFERVESCENCE

I stared at you with lust, pity and loathing,
otherwise known as love:
projecting my fantasies on to your realities,
in the hope of spoiling
this hazy embodiment of desire
with pointless needs.
Another incarnation of immateriality
that becomes a necessity:
demanding some sort of release.

I LOVE YOU, UNFORTUNATELY

I hate you, but there are other factors involved,
unfortunately.
I love your style, your spirit,
even, to some extent, your soul.

You are a warm weight that drags me down,
a black hole that feels unbearably snug.
It's not that you're a bad person,
but I have fallen for you,
and the result is boundless loathing.

Lust is easy, falling in love is easy.
The real challenge is to like somebody:
to not stare into their face
with barely suppressed antagonism
because of the power
you have powerlessly invested in them.

WISHING AND HOPING

I have never been in a relationship,
even when I was enjoying it,
without continually plotting how to get out of it.
And I am not enjoying this.
Lust and loathing are the predominant elements:
desire that transcends incompatibility -
I have no income and you have no patibility -
and the twin poles of suffocation and pining:
Either being smothered half to death with an affection
that I should know better than to take personally,
or craving something I don't want;
and my frequent attempts to view you dispassionately
are never rewarded with the needed indifference
that is your natural domain.
The search for useful flaws is quickly obscured
in a haze of feeling;
I can no longer see beyond the deep surface.
I only wish that the sensuality
would quickly drain out of your features.

LUCKY MAN

As we walked out one night,
my love and I,
I caught a glimpse
of an old bachelor friend
through the window of a restaurant.
He was sitting at the counter,
reading a newspaper over his solitary meal.
He would be going home alone,
getting into bed alone and waking up alone,
rather than returning to a shared bed
with a beautiful woman.
And I felt a sharp pang of envy.
In his aloneness his life seemed fuller, richer,
and less lonely than mine
in its incomplete state of togetherness.
My love also noticed him and turned to me.
"Isn't that your friend?" she said,
"poor guy."

UNKNOWN ROOM, UNKNOWN BED

Temptation is easy to resist
if you're not a receptive, empathetic,
lustful person. It's easy to recoil
in guilt-edged confusion
from the prospect of pleasurable complications.
Temptation is a symptom of allure,
a burden of vitality.
Being a good person:
sounds great... hypothetically.
But what's the point
if you hate every moment of it?
To resist temptation is a sign of weakness
and low character.
You live but once: be brave and fall
into a situation you can't control.

TOXIC FEMININITY

All that can be gained from this is relief.
And that, sadly, is enough:
the suspension of a need
that I would rather kill.

It's what's missing
that keeps me wanting more:
a constant craving for something weak
but irresistible: holding on
to something that's doomed
because I'm holding on to it.

Frustration meets desire halfway.
But at some point, if not satisfied,
it has to subside into superfluity.
This white flame, flickering,
even in these ashes,
the dying embers of a bad habit.

NO HARD FEELINGS

I don't mean to sound ungrateful,
but I wish I'd never met you.

This union has neutered, infantilized,
and almost smothered the life out of me.
It has consigned me to an incomplete and primordial state.
And if I can't summon the strength to end it,
it will be the end of me.

When we met, I felt my life close around me like a soft hell.
You have inspired me
to shut myself down in so many ways;
you have killed my sense of wonder,
and I love you for it.

This lifeline of numbness has sustained my descent,
but it cannot soften the impact.
It has weakened me.
But now, without it, I'd be weaker.

It's over but we're still together,
and I wear the permanent frown of the trapped man:
gritting his remaining teeth in resignation, and sinking them
into a false sense of comfort.

THE RUNOUT GROOVE

Yes, my dear, we have each other:
that's what worries me.
I wouldn't focus on your flaws
if you did not call yourself mine;
you are the living embodiment of my failure,
another symptom of my decline.
But, darling, please don't let our love ever die.
Because if it does, I'll be shattered
by all the time I've wasted
keeping it alive.

ALL MY LOVING

I have a lot more love in me
when I'm not in love,
when one person isn't draining it all.

Love is a new horizon
from which the rest of the world recedes.
It signals the end - of love
and freedom.

But as one grows older,
other possibilities become impractical
and exhausting,
and one has to do something
with one's love.

SATISFACTION

I felt satisfied.
It was an unfamiliar
and unsatisfying sensation.
I wanted it to end.
And it soon did.

ADDENDA

My sense of wonder has dried up and I can't get it up.

The transcendental is strictly off limits.

A perverted form of integrity;
a threadbare urgency,
as pointless as poetry.

My sadness is deeper than yours.

Woke up this morning feeling like the hapless victim of an elaborate
self-defeating plot that I have unwittingly perpetrated against myself.

Non-occupational hazards, obvious temptations.
The tantalizing charms of irritation.

A passing weakness that turned
into a full time occupation.

Meaningful love meaning less lust.

I should have got all this crap out of my system years ago.

a threadbare urgency,
as pointless as poetry.

A 50-year-old man with a come-rag under his pillow.

My life has been dedicated to the pursuit of truth and beauty. Mostly
the former, which, unfortunately, has not been particularly beautiful.

The artist must have the courage of his own impotence.

I have absolutely nothing to say, but I'm not going to let that stop me.

A dry run for disengagement. In search of a satisfying revulsion.

A screen upon which reality scratches
in vain.

To stem the tide of pettiness,
of complaint so engrained.

Lackluster of acuity but acutely lustful.

A spent force of nature, in the service of numbness.

It is hard to give up
giving up. It is hard to give.

I don't care about anybody else's problems. They are not as serious as
mine.

Miserabilist, Declinist, Futilitarian, Negationist, Retreatist, Rejection-
ist.

Latest last excursion into that void.

Regrets: more than a few, too many to mention.

The silence preceding the anticlimax. A pitiful bid for validation or a
claim on eternity.

In celebration of a selfish and lazy existence dedicated to the pursuit
of truth and beauty.

I bought my fatalism, the luxury of alienation.
I bought poverty. Nothing holds me more
than my own assumed tragedy.

How beautiful this would be if I weren't a part of it.

A burst of momentum, squashed. The morning ended up on the floor.

I resent those who have made compromises, and those who haven't had to compromise, and those who have nothing to compromise.

My sadness is deeper than yours. My interior life is richer than yours.

Other people's problems don't interest me, unless they are similar to mine.

Everything's falling apart according to plan.

Bad news: Apparently it's not okay to quit when the going gets tough.

Sometimes floating, usually sinking, the pink cloud dissolves into a red mist.

All this stuff I should have got out of my system years ago, that is still in my so-called system, clogging it up.

Trying to get through life with an open mind and a closed heart. It's an honest struggle.

I've felt like dying, but I've never felt like doing anything about it.

My sadness is not only deeper than yours, but it is wider and in every respect richer.

It used to be that nothing was better than me,
now nothing is better than me.

Your need of me keeps me warm, the way a tea cosy maintains the pot's warmth, long after the tea has lost its flavor.

You have turned masturbation into a luxury for me.

make me wilt.

The run-off from a reservoir of guilt.

Having sex with you is like going to church. I resent the obligation.

From yearning to yawning.

Slouching towards slouching.

My entire life has been dedicated
to the pursuit of truth and beauty.
Mostly the former, which, unfortunately,
has not been particularly beautiful.

Sometimes a spot of masturbation and a brief nap are all a man
needs.

Try dying or die trying.

I am, at least, master of my own downfall.

Stroking the mark where, for years, my elbow has rested, gently scar-
ring the table.

It's not over yet. I haven't definitively failed yet.

A half-life of dishonest struggles and hard-won lies.

From fixed fortifications to mixed mortifications.

Maybe if I sit here for long enough something will emerge.

A necessary dulling of the senses.

Is a slouching woman always less desirable than a slouching man?

I demand recognition for what I imagine I could have done.

And so, lost to myself, I find myself again.

The ceremony, at least, must be honored.

I was on a roll, and I rolled into a rut.

from strange simplicities to crazed complicities.

I have done everything
wrong. That was the plan
all along, to watch other people
move on.

Time that was on my hands
is running through my fingertips
like grains of sand.

I realize now that nothing will ever strike me
with the force of revelation.
And that in itself is a revelation.
It's not much of one
but it will have to do.

Maybe I can be a posthumous failure too.

ABOUT THE AUTHOR

After many years of resistance, John Tottenham finally sold out
to the lucrative, fast-paced world of poetry. He is the author of *The
Inertia Variations*, an epic poetic cycle on the subject of work-avoidance,
indolence and failure, and *Antiepithalamia & Other Poems of Regret and
Resentment*, a sequence of mean-spirited love poems with particular
respect paid to the institution of marriage. His work has been
described as "magnanimous misanthropy," "magical cynicism," and
"an acquired taste that's for everybody." A Londoner by birth,
Tottenham is a long-time resident of Los Angeles.

To give up at last   What a relief